MAKE A MILLION FROM
ONLINE POKER

THE SUREFIRE WAY TO PROFIT FROM THE INTERNET'S COOLEST GAME

NIGEL GOLDMAN

D0003284

JOHN BLAKE

Published by John Blake Publishing Ltd,
3, Bramber Court, 2 Bramber Road,
London W14 9PB, England

www.blake.co.uk

First published in paperback in 2006

ISBN 1 84454 219 X

British Library Cataloguing-in-Publication Data:

A catalogue record for this book is available from the British Library.

Design by www.envydesign.co.uk

Printed in Great Britain by Bookmarque

5 7 9 10 8 6 4

Papers used by John Blake Publishing are natural, recyclable
products made from wood grown in sustainable forests.
The manufacturing processes conform to the environmental
regulations of the country of origin.

Every attempt has been made to contact the relevant copyright-
holders, but some were unobtainable. We would be grateful if the
appropriate people could contact us.

CONTENTS

PREFACE

I DETEST losing at poker more than anything else I've known, just as I love winning more than almost anything else I've ever achieved. I should know: I've gambled since I was ten years old at boarding school, and, since then, I have peaked with 14 million pounds in my bank, and have turned over in excess of 1,000 million pounds playing cards. With such vast experience, I know I can help you make a million from online poker. Some of the secrets revealed in this book have been published for the first time. Many of the world's leading players have attempted to stop publication of them – but, hey, they've had it all their own way for the past few years, so now's the time for the new kids on the block to have a go.

Poker is more a game of skill than of chance. If you lock a professional poker player in a room with an amateur, in the fullness of time the professional will always come out on top. In the short term, a player with a small amount of knowledge and experience can win a tournament, which is what makes the game so attractive, but in the long term the more experienced and skilled players will fare better. That is why the big tournaments all over the world are usually dominated by the same professional players.

Although luck, or chance, does come into play, the mathematical statistics of the game are extremely important. A skilled player will always know what the odds are of hitting a card, and will use that to work out whether or not to call or raise a bet. Good players fold cards early to save their chips, while inexperienced players get involved in pots they should never have considered in the hope of getting lucky – usually an expensive exercise. In this book I will show you how to calculate value – the essential ability you need to succeed at the game. In simple terms, this involves estimating the chance you have of winning a pot and weighing this against the amount of money required to be involved in it. So, if there is £1,000 in the pot, with two players left, and the bet is £200, making the pot £1,200, it will only pay you in the long term to be involved in this pot if you have a better than 6/1 chance of winning. Try to bear this principle in mind while you are reading this book.

The advent of online poker has transformed the game into a billion-pound industry, as has the acceptance and popularity of the Internet- and TV-friendly version of the game, Texas Hold'em. At the heart of the current poker boom, this has outstripped the older and more traditional games such as Five-card Draw and Seven-card Stud.

Although growing in popularity and played every hour of every day, online poker is still, at best, a baby. But it is a baby that is sprouting wings. It is estimated that over $80 billion will be gambled worldwide in 2006 on poker websites. If you type 'poker' into Google, you will get over 44,000,000 hits, which tops the 43,000,000 hits if you type in 'porn'. At any given time, it's estimated that there are over 100,000 people playing poker online in Britain – some from their armchairs at home, many playing professionally, and a fair few earning a good living at it. Many have given up their day jobs to play poker full-time.

This book is designed to assist the beginner and professional alike to master the game. While most top professionals understand the methods I'm going to reveal to you, some don't. And the majority of online second-tier professionals, along with most amateurs, don't seem to understand it at all. To assist you, I've featured three real-life Internet players, following their play over a period of weeks. The true odds and value of hands are clearly detailed and a host of tips revealed, including how to spot and avoid cheats and cheating tables, how to cheat by knowing other players' cards yourself, how to employ a robot to play on the Internet for you and make you money while you sleep, how to make easy money from deposit bonuses on the Internet, and how to win consistently by following an easy betting guideline. I also give details of the best poker sites and many other closely guarded Internet secrets. Finally, I've included the Nigel Goldman guide to the fifteen most important points to remember while playing online.

This book is a must for anybody considering playing poker online.

CHAPTER 1

THE GAME OF POKER

THE GAME OF POKER

POKER is one of the oldest and easiest of all card games to understand. Texas Hold'em, due to its place at the heart of the current Internet boom, is rapidly becoming the most popular form, replacing others such as Five-card Draw and Seven-card Stud. The deal rotates clockwise, hand by hand, the two players to the left of the dealer placing specified '*blinds*' – usually a *small blind*, and a *big blind* (double the small blind) of a predetermined amount of money. In competitions, the blinds go up in value as the competition progresses, making it more and more difficult to accumulate chips.

Each player at the table receives two cards face-down. These are known as 'pocket cards'. There is then a round of betting. Players may fold (put down their hand and take no further part in the round), check-raise (waive the right to bet until a bet has been made by an opponent) and re-raise (equal the amount of the current bet and then increase it) bets during betting rounds. Three cards (known as community cards) are then dealt face-up in the centre of the table. This is called the '*flop*'. Players bet again, and then a fourth community card is dealt (the *turn*). Another round of betting takes place, and then the fifth and final community card is dealt (the *river*). A final betting round takes place. The player who out-bets his opponents, forcing them to fold, or who has the best hand (made up of his pocket cards and three of the community cards) wins the pot. It is vital to learn which pocket cards are valuable – worth betting and raising on – and equally important to appreciate the importance of knowing when to bet and raise. These skills are best acquired as early as possible, but often can take years to master. If you are playing Internet poker for the first time, choose a low blinds table (.05/.10 cents) and only progress to higher blind and pot tables when you are confident you have mastered the basic strategies and have digested all the information in this book. Do not make the costly mistake of initially running up your winnings to ever bigger games. You will inevitably come a cropper when your winning streak evaporates. Keep to sensible levels, and wait until your bankroll has increased sufficiently before taking on the additional risk of playing in a higher-level game or tournament.

2 ♦

2 ♦

CHAPTER 2

TRUE-LIFE INTERNET PLAYERS PROFILED

2 ♦

2 ♦

TRUE-LIFE INTERNET PLAYERS PROFILED

SPENCER CARRINGTON – THE NEW KID ON THE BLOCK

Spencer Carrington is 32 years old and lives in Spain. Formerly a greengrocer in the UK, he has moved from potatoes to poker chips, having been playing online for just over twelve months now. His favourite site is Ladbrokes. I asked him why. 'Good satellite competitions, I know all the players on this site from all over the world, all lads like me. We get on well and send messages to each other during play.' Another reason he favours the Ladbroke site is the tens of thousands of dollars he has deposited there, the rewards

Spencer Carrington

from an afternoon's play in a satellite competition which resulted in him winning a place on the Ladbroke Poker Cruise.

Spencer's handle (the nickname by which all players are known online) is sportsmanspain. It's too long to fit in the name-box provided online, so, should you fancy watching him in action one evening, you'll find it's been abbreviated there to 'sportsmanspa'.

Spencer favours playing in multi-tournaments and always tries to qualify via satellites. He also plays in cash games on the smaller tables ($1/$2) and, like most professionals, plays on four tables at once, using state-of-the-art wireless technology and a 20-inch monitor. 'The best hours to play are on Friday and Saturday evenings. Only European players are allowed to play on the Ladbrokes site, and Friday is usually when most of them have just got paid, been out drinking, come home drunk and logged on. The best time to make a killing is between midnight and 6am on those evenings, when the drunks and inexperienced players are at their most vulnerable.' Unlike a real casino, there is no

11

doorman online to ensure you are of the correct age and sober enough to be admitted.

'But what about a social life?' I asked him innocently.

'You don't have one if you play poker for a living.' The lack of social life is made up for by the huge amount of money Spencer has accumulated in a short period of time, and the glitzy competitions he qualifies for all over the world, which, for him, are better than a holiday.

Spencer can tell who the drunk or high players are at any table online by the way they bluff. He writes copious notes about all the players he meets and plays against. Electronic notepads are provided for this on all the major poker sites. 'Get to know your opponents,' Spencer muses. 'They all have methods and "tells" online which you need to be aware of and use to your maximum advantage.' Spencer is obviously taking his online gaming very seriously. His longest session so far is fourteen hours without a break. He regularly makes $1,000–$2,000 during such marathons, with his biggest win for an evening being around $5,000. He's had his setbacks, too, of course. They are known as 'bad beats' in the trade. 'I was playing in the European Championships in the spring of 2005 and was lying in twelfth place out of 480 entries, and was sitting there with around 100,000 chips. I went all-in with pocket Kings, and got called by pocket Tens. My opponent hit a Ten on the river to knock me out.'

By far the most important point in his poker career to date has been qualifying for the Ladbroke's Poker cruise. Satellites had been running for twenty weeks on ladbrokespoker.com. Spencer played repeatedly to qualify for this valuable place that was on offer, and his persistence paid off when he won it. He got a free seat on the Poker cruise, worth $7,500 in entry fees alone – a major achievement given that thousands of players had tried and failed to win this coveted prize.

Spencer was now the new kid on the block. The tournament itself followed a unique format devised by Ladbrokes Head of Poker, David Tarbet. The field was to be split into four groups, with each group playing down to nine players. The final nine from each group carried their chips forward to the semi-final stages of thirty-six players. These thirty-six then played down to a final table of six and again carried their chips forward. The structure was slow throughout, with about ten hours of play in the group stages and reduced blinds at the last thirty-six and final table to allow a greater amount of play. Many players commented on how fair the structure was, and the tournament ran like clockwork under the expert supervision of Thomas Kremser of the IPF. The first night of the cruise saw a welcome cocktail party and grand draw ceremony almost as elaborate as a football World Cup draw. Just as there almost always seems to be a 'group of death' in the World Cup so it proved here, with pre-tournament favourites Dave 'Devilfish' Ulliott, Poker Million Champ Donnacha O'Dea, and Lucy Rokach – fresh from a $50,000 win at the Vic – all thrown into Group A.

The 'group of death' tag rang true for both O'Dea and Ulliott, who both headed for the nearest cash game, but not so for Rokach, who carried a very healthy stack of 28,300 through to the last thirty-six. Also through from group A was Brian 'cresta' Medley, who was the older half of a father-and-son team that had qualified for the cruise. Ireland's Paddy O'Connor, who finished thirty-eighth in this year's WSOP main event, also made the semi-finals on day one.

Back home in Spain, Spencer's friends, family and admirers had been busy mopping up the 150/1 each way on Spencer offered by Ladbrokes – odds that soon started to look generous. Though nothing much happened for him during the first hour or so of the competition, Spencer then started getting some good hands, played well and wound up with $37,000 in chips and in the running. Ladbrokes weren't slow to notice the quality of his play, either, and quickly slashed his odds to 80/1.

Day two, and Spencer got his chips up to 300,000 twice. After nipping out for a cigarette, he came back to pocket Aces, followed this with a re-raise from an AK and, after a few near misses, he wound up with 135,000 at the end of play to go into day three in second position. Ladbrokes slashed his odds again, this time to 11/4. On day three, he played tight and finished the day with 145,000, a ten-grand improvement, going into the final on day four still in second place and with everything to play for. Participants on the cruise were invited to bid for the winning player by betting on who they thought would win the competition, and Spencer, having made many good friends on the boat, proved his popularity, receiving more bids than anyone else.

Then, as he walked into the poker lounge for the final, the magnitude of the task ahead hit him. For the first time he felt nervous. On the table in front of him was 700,000 in US dollars (at that stage, he didn't know it was moody money for the cameras!). And worse, a huge projector screen was right in his face broadcasting every hand. The famous TV player Dave Ulliott (Devilfish) wished Spencer luck with the words: 'any hand can win'.

This was Spencer's first live tournament, and, sensibly, he decided to do a deal with the chip leader, Londoner Eric 'Lowball' Dalby, arranging to save some of the prize money for the winner who came second. At 74, Eric was the oldest player in the field, but he outlasted 208 of his peers, some of whom were over fifty years younger, to capture the $250,000 first prize. Who said poker's a young man's game? Spencer bagged $160,000, $135,000 from Messrs Ladbrokes and Co., and $25,000 saved with the finalist, who Spencer confirmed 'wouldn't have done a deal with anyone else'. Good work if you can get it.

Online, Spencer continues to progress. Often playing in Sunday-lunchtime competitions, he anticipates playing poker for a living within the next five years. And his advice to would-be poker professionals – play lots of small games, treat it as a business, keep 100 times what you are playing for in your poker bank and only play good hands. Spencer has invested his money wisely, using some of it to start his own poker website and opening a swish private members poker club in Spain.

MARK DOUGLAS GRIFFIN

Mark is 44 years old and from Weston-super-Mare. In his previous life in the UK, he was a

Mark Douglas Griffin

manager/partner at Kentucky Fried Chicken, before buying a couple of pubs. He moved to Spain in 1999, and opened a bar in the fashionable area of Benalmadena. He used to be a punter, but soon realised that when betting on horses the odds were stacked against him, so about three years ago he decided to become a bookmaker, bought an existing sports lounge and has never looked back. Having successfully played poker, brag, backgammon and casino games for reasonable stakes, he first discovered live poker in 2000, when he and a few friends would get together after racing in a bar called the Winning Post where they would play reasonable-stakes games. 'After about six weeks, nobody would play me for money,' he commented wryly.

In 2003, the Winning Post boys invited him back to play the new version of Texas Hold'em. He played five or six games and won those, too. Then another bar started running proper poker competitions. Mark got involved, kept winning and was hooked, going on to discover Internet poker in November 2004. Although he's explored various sites, including Pacific, Party Poker, William Hill and Ladbrokes, his favourite is Paradise Poker, not only because they have good games and excellent satellites, but also because he finds the people on that site friendly – he has made many friends online, and even met one of his oppos in person when he turned up át Mark's sports lounge in Spain. Mark's handle on Paradise, by the way, is 'Betdempseys'.

When he started playing in November 2004, Mark didn't even have a credit card in Spain, so he got together with his son Robin and racing-odds compiler and form student Craig Cairnes to play on Paradise's free ten-man competitions. The first of three to win received a tenner from the other two! Naturally, Mark cleaned up, again. He started playing for real money online in January 2005. Commencing with $5 ten-man tournaments, with $25 going to the winner, he very quickly went to the front, and was soon playing in $10, then $20, competitions, always at ten-man tables. In February, he discovered satellite qualifiers for big competitions. Beginning with a $6 satellite, he won a $200

WPT seat as a late qualifier from 100 players. He ended up in a competition with 600 players, the top five finishers winning a $25,000 WPT seat. Mark finished sixth, got $1,000 for his trouble, but was still gutted. He then went on to win a $1,200 turbo competition and an $800 hammock, putting him a couple of thousand up in cash games.

By now, Mark was convinced that his play was sufficiently tight and skilled for him to win something substantial any minute. He obtained a seat cheaply via satellite for an online $100,000 competition being staged that March on the Paradise site and finished 200 out of 600 players, having hugely enjoyed the experience. The following Sunday, he managed to qualify for a seat in another $100,000+ competition for a mere $5 entry fee. The tournament commenced at 11pm, and Mark had already made up his mind to play tight. 'The early parts of these competitions are when one mustn't get tempted to play loose.' After the first hour, there was no change in his chip stack, and by the end of the second hour he had seen a couple of hands and was lying 150th out of the 300 players remaining, the other 300 having dropped out. During the third hour, he continued to maintain his chip position and, by the start of the fourth, another 150 players having been knocked out, he was in seventy-fifth place. 'Throughout this tournament, I always seemed to be lying in the middle of the pack,' Mark recalls. Just after the fifth hour, he made it to the final table, by which time it was 4am in the morning. There were now only ten players left and Mark, amazingly, was sitting in fifth place – still in the middle of the pack. He was going well, to say the least, with something in the region of $70,000–80,000 in chips in front of him, the table chip leader sitting with 200,000. Three more players went out, leaving just seven. Mark, now on the big blind, got dealt AK spades and, understandably, was becoming increasingly excited. Of the remaining players, all folded except one – a Swede called Johan (handle Dubbletommate) – who committed all-in. Mark called the all-in bet, knowing that if the worst came to the worst and he was out he would still finish seventh and pick up $4,000. The cards were exposed, and to Mark's dismay Johan has pocket Aces, which gave Mark just a 22 per cent chance of winning.

The situation didn't look good, and it was clear that he needed a hefty slice of luck. The flop came: spade, spade, nothing. Then the turn: nothing. Finally, the river: spade. Mark has made a nuts flush on the river and went straight into second place on the leaderboard. Left short-stacked, Johan was soon out, whereupon Mark decided to play like granite, and wait for monsters. Soon there were only two players left: Mark, sitting with 290,000, and 'Billybob' with 600,000. The blinds were going up, and Mark was desperate to double up to put himself in the running. His chance came when he saw A8 clubs in the hole – referred to as 'dead man's hand'. His opponent had K10. The flop, turn and river produced nothing for either player, and Mark's A8 held up. The positions were thus reversed, Mark now sitting with 600,000 while Billybob's stack had been reduced to 290,000. After a couple more hands, Billybob went all-in with K10, which Mark called, quite correctly, with A6 off-suit. The flop brought 10xx (ragrag), the turn an Ace; and the river nothing. Game over. Mark had won, and walked away with a cheque for a cool $38,650.

Mark is now absolutely convinced that he can make good money playing poker for a living and, if the past few months are anything to go by, I'd have to agree with him. Over coffee in the gardens of the Torrequebrada Hotel, on the Costa del Sol, in June 2005, I asked Mark what he feels are the important factors in his success as a poker player, and what advice he would give to new players coming in on the scene for the first time. A major advantage, he believes, is knowledge of odds compilation, and that, probably, is why bookmakers, market makers and ex-City traders tend to fare well at the game. Mark also believes that one's position on the table (in relation to the dealer button) is also vitally important. Invaluable to him also has been the considerable help and advice he's received from a professional poker-player friend called Thai, from Canada, who he met in his sports lounge. Having played Limit Hold'em online for five years, Thai helped Mark considerably with strategy. Oh yes, and there's one bit of advice from Mark for would-be poker beginners: 'Don't bluff!' And, if you must, for heaven's sake don't let your opponent catch you at it!

MICHAEL SENKER – THE SILVER FOX

Michael started playing poker online when a professional sportsman friend of his was sponsored by Empire Poker to go online and play a tournament. The friend couldn't play poker so asked Michael to play for him in his office. 'I knew the rudiments of the game,' says Michael, 'but had never played online before. Anyway, I played the tournament for my friend, got knocked out right away, but instantly got the bug! At the time I was in the video business, I was bored at work and was about to sell out, so I used to sit in my office playing eight hours a day online for play money on Empire Poker's site. At work, I would meet up online with mates, a little social club as I called it, and then I would go home and play all night! I did this

Michael Senker – the Silver Fox

for about a year, playing twelve hours a day, seven days a week – living at home with my long-suffering wife. I admit to spending every waking minute playing poker online.' At work, his addiction was starting to become a problem – he would be in a meeting with a rep while at the same time playing poker. The buzz of being in a million-pound pot was incredibly exciting, even though the money wasn't for real but merely play money (used in free games to get people started, 'winnings' being accumulated in play chips with no real value). He admits he didn't want to go out. 'I only wanted to play poker online or watch it being played on TV, read about poker or talk about poker! This started to affect my social life – I used to go to Vegas on business trips, but the hotel I pitched up at didn't have a poker room, so within minutes of arriving in Vegas I found myself in Binions.' There he found himself in a game where men could lose ten grand to each other and the house couldn't win it all. Back at his hotel room, he would stay up most of the night playing online, still for fun money, still addicted, still learning all the nuances of the game, not quite confident enough to play for real just yet, but getting there: practising, perfecting, become more skilful and dangerous, like a sly fox. Then, after eighteen months of slog online, he decided to play for real money.

'What was your first concern?' I asked him.

'At first I didn't trust the sites,' Michael commented. 'How was I going to get paid? I didn't have to worry about it, though, because I never won! ... I'm not really a gambler now; I did all that when I was young – horses and so forth. Now I'm more disciplined, and treat poker like a business ... I started pretending that my play money was real, and began playing differently to everyone else – trap checking, folding bad hands early – and I built my play money account up to 30 million! So I started playing with real money. Mistake! After opening my first credit-card account online with Empire, I pumped in a hundred to five hundred dollars a day over the first few weeks; up, down. I won a $200 tourney, got to a thousand, and then immediately played another five tourneys.

I can't play multi-tables – I'm just not quick enough – so I was plodding on, getting nowhere. But I was trying to learn: playing five to seven hours a day and buying just about every book on poker I could find! ... I realised quite early on that there is a dark side to the Internet, many pros walking around the net looking for a "fish". The "find a player lobby" should be renamed "find a fish", for the lobby louts are constantly waiting to pounce.

'I finally decided that my losses thus far had to be dealt with philosophically, not that they were huge. I thought of them as a kind of joining-up fee, very similar to what you'd pay for joining a golf club and buying all the necessary golf equipment. To my mind, I was getting going, even though I was still losing money. I probably lost between seven and eight thousand pounds during those eighteen months, but in the long term that was to prove of tremendous value.

'I then decided to play only tournaments – and where better than Las Vegas? So off I went with some friends, and decided to play at the Venetian and the Mirage. The Mirage had just opened their poker room and things were a bit disorganised, so I went to another casino next door — "Hurrahs", I think it was called — which had a small poker room where you could go and learn. There were some games I wasn't familiar with, so I sat down with a few players, still all dressed up to the nines for the Venetian — white cap, dark glasses — like some "Big Charlie" hitting Vegas. I was there to gain experience, and I learned quickly. Looking round the table, I spotted this old geezer with thick glasses and a slightly tilted baseball cap, his total vocabulary seeming to comprise pass/fold. He's what's known in the trade as a rock. I promise you, he didn't play a hand for an hour and a quarter! I wondered for a moment if he'd come in from the cold, and then thought maybe he was in for the free drinks and buffet. Everyone around was busy betting, calling, raising and generally getting involved, apart from this man, but, then suddenly, after a large bet, I heard the shout: "POT!" Well, being of a certain age, my first thought was that he'd been caught short and a nurse was going to appear any moment with a bedpan! Next thing I heard was a voice calling $800 or some such. It was *me*, unable to resist the challenge – remember, this guy hasn't said anything for over two hours by then, so I should have realised he must have some sort of hand. The flop produced J8rag (Jack, Eight, and useless card), the turn a Jack, and there he was with a full house JJJ88. It taught me a hard lesson – and that's why I play with a Mirage $1 chip as my card guard, which is all I walked out with that night, and a salutary reminder that I'm not as good as I might like to think. I didn't actually walk out; I stood around for a few hours observing, and saw some very old pros just waiting for fish. They just sit there and win fortunes – three, four, five grand a week. Then there are the great players who can sit at a table and only play one hand an hour; only, that is, when they have the nuts. I learned a lot in Vegas, learned more online and then came to Spain. I treat my poker like a business, now.'

CHAPTER 3

HOW TO VALUE POCKET CARDS

HOW TO VALUE
POCKET CARDS

IN online poker, 10 per cent of the players win 90 per cent of the money in the long run. Always remember that most online players are bad. Seldom do anything fancy, you don't need to! Most of your profit will come from doing the obvious correct moves.

The foundation of Texas Hold'em is the starting hand (pocket cards). Learn and memorise by heart which of these are valuable. This is the solid foundation for successful play. Beginners make the fundamental mistake of seeing far too many flops. To win consistently, you should see only about 20 per cent of the flops. If you discipline yourself to see only these, you will find yourself playing very tight with substantial pocket cards. Good players do most of their gambling on the flop. This is the key to success at online poker. Guard this information carefully; it's your passport to riches!

Here's a list to assist you in ranking pocket cards.

- Group A: AA KK – always raise pre-flop
- Group B: QQ JJ AK (suited) – always raise pre-flop
- Group C: TT AK AQ (suited), AJ (suited), KQ (suited) – always bet/call
- Group D: AQ 99 AT (suited), KJ (suited), QJ (suited), KT (suited), late position – use judgement
- Group E: 88 AJ KQ QT (suited), A9 (suited), JT (suited), AT A8 (suited), late position – use judgement
- Group F: KJ 77 QJ KT QT JT A7 (suited), K9 (suited), Q9 (suited), T9 (suited), J9 (suited), late position – use judgement
- Group G: KJ 77 QJ KT QT JT A7 (suited), K9 (suited), Q9 (suited), T9 (suited), J9

(suited), late position – use judgement
- Group H: 66 55 44 33 22 A5 (suited), A6 (suited), A4 (suited), A3 (suited), A2 (suited), late position – use judgement
- Group I A9 K9 98 (suited), 87 (suited), 76 (suited) – possible, if value
- All other cards: FOLD

CHAPTER 4

CALCULATING POKER ODDS

CALCULATING POKER ODDS

THE following pages involve a bit of maths. When working with odds and probabilities (just like a bookmaker or a city spread trader), you will be required to know at least some elementary arithmetic. Now, while I sympathise with those who are bad at maths and prefer to avoid it, if that's you then you're not cut out for playing poker. Should you choose simply to memorise your odds for each type of hand, so be it, but the person who can calculate odds in an instant will be a far better player in the long run. Even in beginners' guides to Texas Hold'em, odds are stressed as a fundamental foundation for the solid poker player.

HAND ODDS AND POKER ODDS

Hand odds are the chances of you making a hand in Texas Hold'em poker. For example, if you hold two hearts and there are two hearts on the flop, your hand odds for making a flush are about two to one (2:1). This means that approximately every three times you play this hand you will hit your flush one of those times. If your hand odds are 3:1, then you would hit your hand one out of every four times; in other words, there's a 25 per cent chance. The formula to learn is as follows:

X to 1 odds = You hit your hand one out of (X + 1) times

X to 1 odds = 100 / (X + 1) = percentage chance to hit your hand

The table below sets out your percentage chance and odds of hitting an out by the river:

Outs	Flop %	Turn %	Flop odds	Turn odds	Draw type
2	8	4	12	22	Pocket pair → set
3	13	7	7	14	Single overcard draw
4	17	9	5	10	Gutshot, two pair → full house
5	20	11	4	8	One pair → two pair or set, gutshot +backdoor
6	24	13	3.2	6.7	No pair → pair, two overcard draw
7	28	15	2.6	5.6	Set → full house or better (not counting extra turn outs)
8	32	17	2.2	4.7	Open straight draw
9	35	19	1.9	4.1	Flush draw, open +backdoor draw
10	42	22	1.6	3.6	
11	42	24	1.4	3.2	
12	45	26	1.2	2.8	Flush+gutshot draw
13	48	28	1.1	2.5	
14	51	30	0.95	2.3	
15	54	33	0.85	2.1	Flush+open draw
16	57	34	0.75	1.9	Flush+open +one overcard
17	60	37	0.66	1.7	

To calculate your hand odds, you first need to know how many *outs* your hand has. Outs are defined as cards in the deck that help you make your hand. So, if you hold AK of spades and have two spades on the flop, that leaves nine more spades in the deck, since there are thirteen cards of each suit. This means you have nine outs to complete your flush – *though this is not necessarily the best hand.* Usually, you want your outs to count towards a nut draw, but this is not always possible. The quick among you might be wondering, 'But what if someone else is holding a spade, doesn't that decrease my outs?' The answer is yes and no. If you know for sure that someone else is holding a spade, then you will have to count that against your total odds. In most situations, however, when you do not know what your opponents hold, you can only do calculations with the knowledge that is available to you. That knowledge is your pocket cards and the cards on the table. So, in essence, you are doing the calculations as if you were the only person at the table, in which case, there are nine spades left in the deck.

When calculating outs, it's also important not to overcount your odds. An example would be a flush draw in addition to an open straight draw, as shown below:

Example 1: You hold J♣ T♣ and the board shows 8♣ Q♣ K♠. A Nine or Ace gives you a straight (8 outs), while any club gives you the flush (9 outs). However, you don't want to count the Ace of clubs and Nine of clubs twice towards your straight draw and flush draw. The true number of outs, therefore, is actually fifteen (8 outs + 9 outs ? 2 outs) instead of seventeen (8 outs + 9 outs). In addition to this, sometimes an out isn't really a true out. Imagine, for example, you're chasing an open-ended straight draw when two of another suit are on the table. In this case, where you would normally have eight total outs to hit your straight, two of those outs will result in three to a suit on the table. This makes a possible flush for your opponents. As a result, you really only have six outs for a nut straight draw.

Another more complex situation is illustrated below:

Example 2: You hold J82 and the flop comes 9TJ rainbow (i.e. all of a different suit). To make a straight, you need a Queen or Seven to drop, giving you four outs each or a total of eight outs. *But*, you have to look at the situation if a Queen comes, because the board will then show 9TJQ. This means that anyone holding a King will have made a King-high straight, while you hold the dominated (that is, beaten by your opponent) Queen-high straight. So the only card that can really help you is the Seven, which gives you four outs, or the equivalent of a gutshot draw (i.e. a straight missing one inside card). While it's true that someone might not be holding the King (especially in a short or heads-up game), in a big game, it's a very scary position to be in.

HOW TO CALCULATE HAND ODDS
(THE LONGER WAY)

Once you know how to count correctly the number of outs you have on a hand, you can use that to calculate what percentage of the time you will hit your hand by the river. Probability can be calculated easily for a single event, like the flipping of the river card from the turn. This would simply be: total outs/remaining cards. For two cards, however, say the turn and river, it's a bit trickier. This is calculated by figuring the probability of your cards not hitting twice in a row. This can be calculated as shown below:

Flop to river % = 1 − [((47 − Outs) / 47) x ((46 − Outs) / 46)]

Turn to river % = 1 − [(46 − Outs) / 46]

The number 47 represents the remaining cards left in the deck after the flop (52 total cards, minus 2 in your hand and 3 on the flop = 47 remaining cards). Even though there might not technically be 47 cards remaining, you should calculate as though you are the only player in the game. To illustrate, here is a two-overcard draw (an overcard being a card higher than any on the board), which has three outs for each overcard, giving a total of six outs for a top pair draw:

Two overcard draw = $1 - [(47 - 6) / 47$ x $(46 - 6) / 46]$

= $1 - [(41/47)$ x $(40/46)]$

= $1 - [0.87$ x $0.87]$

= $1 - 0.76$

= 0.24

= 24% chance to draw overcards from flop to river

To change a percentage to odds, the formula is: odds = (1 / percentage) - 1. Thus, to change the 24 per cent draw into odds, we do the following:

Odds = (1 / 24% two overcard draw) - 1

= (1 / 0.24) - 1

= 4.17 - 1

= 3.17 or approx 3.2

HOW TO CALCULATE HAND ODDS (THE SHORTER WAY)

Now that you've learned the proper way of calculating hand odds in Texas Hold'em, there is a shortcut that makes it much easier to calculate odds. After you find the number of outs you have, multiply by four and you will get a close estimate to the percentage of hitting that hand from the flop. Multiply by two, instead, to get a percentage estimate from the turn. You can see how this works from the figures below, taken from the table presented earlier under 'Hand odds and poker odds'.

Outs	Flop %	Turn %	Flop odds	Turn odds	Draw type
4	17	9	5	10	Gutshot, two pair → full house
5	20	11	4	8	One pair → two pair or set, gutshot + backdoor
6	24	13	3.2	6.7	No pair → pair, two overcard draw
7	28	15	2.6	5.6	Set → full house or + (not counting extra turn outs)

As you can see, this is a much easier method of finding your percentage odds. But what about ratio odds? This is still done using the formula: odds = (1 / percentage) - 1. However, we can rephrase this maths equation so that your brain can process it a little more easily: odds = (100 / whole percentage) - 1. Using 100 divided by the whole percentage number, such as 24 per cent, we can easily see that 100/24 is equal to about 4. Take away 1 from that and you get a rough estimate of the odds, at about 3:1. Let's try this all the way through from the beginning.

You hold: A♣ J♠. The flop is: 5♣ T♦ K♦. Total outs are: Queen gutshot (4) plus Ace overcard (3) minus Q or Ad (2) which equals 5. The percentage for the draw is five outs times four, which equals 20 per cent. The odds, therefore, are (100 / 20) minus 1, which equals 5, minus 1 again, which equals 4:1. Odds of 4:1 mean that you will make your draw one out of every five times.

If the one out of five doesn't make sense to you, think about the 1:1 odds of flipping heads or tails on a coin. You'll flip heads 50 per cent of the time, so one out of every two times it'll come heads. The formula to remember is: X:1 hand odds means that you'll hit 1 out of every X+1 times.

POT ODDS AND POKER ODDS

Now that you know how to calculate poker odds in terms of hand odds, you're probably wondering what you're going to need this skill for. That's a good question. This is where pot odds come into play.

Pot odds are simply a ratio of the amount of money in the pot compared with how much money it takes to call. If there is $100 in the pot and it takes $10 to call, your pot odds are 100:10, or 10:1. If there is $50 in the pot and it takes $10 to call, then your pot odds are 50:10 or 5:1. The higher the ratio, the better your pot odds are. The formula in this case is as follows: X:1 pot odds means that you must win this hand 1 out of X+1 times to break even.

Pot odds ratios are very useful in gauging how often you need to win a hand to break even. If there is $100 in the pot and it takes $10 to call, you must win this hand 1 out of eleven times in order to break even. The thinking goes along the lines of: if you play eleven times, it'll cost you $110, but when you win, you get $110 ($100 + your $10 call).

The usefulness of hand odds and pot odds becomes very apparent when you start comparing the two. As we now know, in a flush draw, your *hand odds* for making your flush are 1.9:1. Let's say you're in a hand with a nut flush draw and it's $5 to you on the flop to call. Do you call? Your answer should be: *What are my pot odds?* If there is $15 in the pot plus a $5 bet from an opponent, then you are getting 20:5 or 4:1 pot odds. This means that, in order to break even, you must win one out of every five times. However, with your flush draw, your odds of winning are one out of every three times! You should quickly realise that not only are you breaking even, but also you're making a nice profit on this. Let's calculate the profit margin by theoretically playing this hand 100 times from the flop, when it's then checked to the river.

Net cost to play = 100 hands x $5 to call
= –$500

Pot value = $15 + $5 bet + $5 call

Odds to win = 1.9:1 or 35% (from
the flop)

Total hands won = 100 x odds to win
(35%) = 35 wins

Net profit = net cost to play + (total times
won x pot value)

= –$500 + (35 x $25)

= –$500 + $875

= $375 profit

As you can see, you have a great reason to play this flush draw, because you'll be making money in the long run according to your hand odds and pot odds. The most fundamental point to take from this is: if your pot odds are greater than your hand odds, then you are making a profit. So, even though you may be faced with a gutshot straight draw at times, which is a terrible draw at 5:1 hand odds, it can be worth calling if you are getting pot odds greater than 5:1. On the other hand, if you have an excellent draw such as the flush draw, but someone has just raised a large amount so that your pot odds are 1:1 for instance, then you obviously should not continue trying to draw to a flush, as you will lose money in the long run. In this situation, a fold or semi-bluff is your only solution, unless you know there will be callers behind you who improve your pot odds to better than break even.

Your ability to memorise or calculate your hand odds and figure out your pot odds will lead you to make many right decisions in the future. Just be sure to remember that fundamental principle of playing drawing hands when your pot odds are greater than your hand odds.

POKER ODDS FROM THE FLOP TO TURN AND TURN TO RIVER

An important point I need to make here – and one that many players who otherwise understand Hold'em odds tend to forget – is that a good part of the theoretical odds calculations from the flop to the river *assumes there is no betting on the turn*. So, while it's true that the odds for completing a flush draw are

1.9:1, you can only call a 1.9:1 pot on the flop if your opponent will let you see both the turn and river cards for one call. Unfortunately, most of the time, this will not be the case, so you should not calculate pot odds from the flop to the river, but instead calculate them one card at a time. To do this, simply use the same odds that you have going from the turn to the river. So, for example, your odds of hitting a flush from the turn to the river are 4:1, which means that your odds of hitting a flush from the flop to the turn are 4:1 as well.

To help illustrate further, I give two examples below of calculating a flush, showing, in turn, incorrect and correct ways of thinking.

An example of incorrect pot odds maths
Single hand
You hold: flush draw
Flop: $10 pot + $10 bet
You call: $10 (getting 2:1 odds)
Turn: $30 pot + $10 bet
You call: $10 (getting 4:1 odds)

Long-term results over 100 hands
Cost to play = 100 hands x ($10 flop call + $10 turn call) = $2,000
Total won = 100 hands x 35% chance to win x $50 pot = $1,750
Total net = $1,750 (won) - $2,000 (cost) = -$250 profit = - $2.5/hand

An example of correct pot odds maths
Single hand
You hold: flush draw
Flop: $30 pot + $10 bet
You call: $10 (getting 4:1 odds)
Turn: $50 pot + $16 bet
You call: $16 (getting about 4:1 odds)

Long-term results over 100 hands
Cost to play = 100 hands x ($10 flop call + $16 turn call) = $2,600
Total won = 100 hands x 35% chance to win x $82 pot = $2,870
Total net = $2,870 (won) - $2,600 (cost) = $270 profit = $2.7/hand

As you can see from these example calculations, calling a flush draw with 2:1 pot odds on the flop can lead to a long-term loss, if there is additional betting past the flop. Most of the time, however, there is a concept called 'implied value' (which we'll get to next) that is able to help flush draws and open-ended straight draws still remain profitable even with seemingly 'bad' odds. The draws that you want to worry about the most are your long-shot draws: overcards, gutshots and two outers (hoping to make a set with your pocket pair). If you draw these hands using incorrect odds (such as flop to river odds), you will be severely punished in the long run.

IMPLIED VALUE

Implied value is a cool concept that takes into account future betting. Like the above section, where you have to worry about your opponent betting on the turn, implied value most often is used to anticipate your opponent calling on the river. So, for example, let's say you have yet another flush draw and are being offered 3:1 pot odds on the turn. Knowing that you need 4:1

pot odds to make this a profitable call, you decide to fold.

Aha, but wait! Here is where implied value comes into play. Even though you're getting 3:1 pot odds on the turn, you can likely anticipate your opponent calling you on the river if you do hit your flush draw. This means that, even though you're only getting 3:1 pot odds, since you anticipate your opponent calling a bet on the river, you are anticipating 4:1 pot odds – so you're able to make this call on the turn.

Understood from a practical standpoint, then, implied value usually means that you can take one bet off your drawing odds on the turn, in anticipation of your opponents calling at least one bet. In some more advanced areas, you can use implied odds as a means of making some draws that might not usually be profitable, but that stand to make big payouts when they do hit. For example, if you're known as a tight player, you might draw to a gutshot against another tight player. Even though this is horribly bad play (but hopefully one that won't prove too costly), it can pay off if you know your opponent in all likelihood won't believe you've played anything so risky. Personally, I wouldn't recommend fancy implied-odds plays like these, but I mention them so that you'll be alert to players attempting to pull the ploy on you.

PROBABILITIES – WHAT MOST PROS DON'T KNOW!

In this section I give the probabilities (in terms of odds and percentages) of *being dealt* various combinations, and then of improving them. They should help you to know what to do pre-flop in a Hold'em poker match. Remember, though, that they are just odds. Just because you're facing a favourable percentage doesn't mean you're assured of a win.

THE DEAL

The probability of being dealt various combinations is as follows:

- Pocket Bullets (A-A): 220/1 (0.45%)
- Any pocket pair: 16/1 (5.9%)
- A-K suited: 331/1 (0.3%)

- A-K off-suit: 110/1 (0.9%)
- A-K suited or off-suit: 82/1 (1.2%)
- Any two suited cards: 3.3/1 (24%)
- Max stretch suited connectors; J-T suited: 46/1 (2.1%)
- Max stretch connectors; J-T suited or off-suit: 11/1 (8.5%)
- Either Pocket Bullets (A-A) or Big Dogs (K-K): 110/1 (0.9%)
- Either Pocket Bullets (A-A), Big Dogs (K-K) or Big Slick (A-K): 46/1 (2.1%)
- Either Pocket Bullets (A-A), Big Dogs (K-K), Big Slick (A-K), Pocket Ladies (Q-Q), A-Q or K-Q: 19/1 (5%)
- Any pocket pair or two cards of Ten or higher: 4.5/1 (18%)
- Any pocket pair of Sevens or higher or two cards of Ten or higher: 5.4/1 (16%)

NB: If you take a pocket pair to the river, you have a 4.2/1 (19%) chance of making a set or better. If you take two suited cards to the river, you have a 15/1 (6.4%) chance of making a flush in your suit by then. Your chance of making a flush in your suit by the river with two unsuited cards is 53/1 (1.8%).

THE FLOP

The probability of improving to a set or better from a pocket pair is 7.5/1 (11.8%), which can broken down as follows:

- A set: 8.3/1 (10.8%)
- A full house: 36/1 (0.74%)
- Quads 407/1: (0.25%)
- A flush from two suited cards: 118/1 (0.84%)
- A four-flush from two suited cards: 8.1/1 (10.9%)
- A three-flush from two suited cards: 1.4/1 (41.6%)
- A four-flush from one suited card: 88/1 (1.1%)
- A three-flush from one suited card: 6.8/1 (12.8%)
- A straight from two max stretch connectors: 76/1 (1.3%)
- An eight outs (open-ended or double belly buster) straight draw from two max stretch connectors: 8.6/1 (10.5%)

- A gutshot straight draw from two max stretch connectors: 3.6/1 (22%)
- At least a pair (using your pocket cards) from two non-pair cards: 2.1/1 (32.4%)
- A pair (using one of your pocket cards) from two non-pair cards: 2.5/1 (29%)
- Two pair (using both of your pocket cards) from two non-pair cards: 49/1 (2%)
- Any two pair from two non-pair cards: 24/1 (4%)
- Trips (using one of your pocket cards) from two non-pair cards: 73/1 (1.35%)
- A full house (using both of your pocket cards) from two non-pair cards: 1087/1 (0.09%)
- Quads (using one of your pocket cards) from two non-pair cards: 9799/1 (0.01%)

Listed below is the probability of various combinations appearing on the three flop cards:

- Three of a kind: 424/1 (0.24%)
- A pair: 5/1 (17%)
- Three suited cards: 18/1 (5.2%)
- Two suited cards: 0.8/1 (55%)
- No suited cards (rainbow): 1.5/1 (40%)

- Three cards in sequence: 28/1 (3.5%)
- Two cards in sequence: 1.5/1 (40%)
- No cards in sequence: 0.8/1 (56%)

FROM FLOP TO TURN

The following shows the probabilities of improving your hand from the flop to the turn:

- A full house or better from a set on the next card (7 outs): 5.7/1 (15%)
- A full house from two pair on the next card (4 outs): 11/1 (9%)
- A set from one pair on the next card (2 outs): 23/1 (4.3%)
- A flush from a four-flush on the next card (9 outs): 4.2/1 (19%)
- A straight from an open-ended straight draw on the next card (8 outs): 4.9/1 (17%)
- A straight from a gutshot straight draw on the next card (4 outs): 11/1 (9%)
- A pair from two non-pair cards (over cards) on the next card (6 outs): 6.8/1 (13%)
- A second pair with your kicker on the next card, when you hold the same pair as your opponent but are 'out kicked' (3 outs): 15/1 (6%)

FROM FLOP TO RIVER

The following shows the probabilities of improving your hand from the flop to the river:

- A full house or better from a set by the river: 2/1 (33%)
- A full house or better from two pair by the river (4 outs): 5.1/1 (17%)
- A set or better from one pair by the river (2 outs): 11/1 (8.4%)
- A flush from a four-flush by the river (9 outs): 1.9/1 (35%)
- A flush from a three-flush by the river: 23/1 (4.2%)
- A straight from an open-ended straight draw by the river (8 outs): 2.2/1 (32%)
- A straight from a gutshot straight draw by the river (4 outs): 5.1/1 (17%)
- A pair or better from two non-pair cards (overcards) by the river (6 outs): 3.2/1 (24%)
- A second pair with your kicker by the river, when you hold the same pair as your opponent but are 'out kicked' (3 outs): 7/1 (13%)

FROM TURN TO RIVER

The following shows the probabilities of improving your hand from the turn to the river:

- A full house or better from a set on the final card (10 outs): 3.6/1 (22%)
- A full house from two pair on the final card (4 outs): 11/1 (9%)
- A set from one pair on the final card (2 outs): 22/1 (4.4%)
- A flush from a four-flush on the final card (9 outs): 4.1/1 (20%)
- A straight from an open-ended straight draw on the final card (8 outs): 4.8/1 (17%)
- A straight from a gutshot straight draw on the final card (4 outs): 11/1 (9%)
- A pair from two non-pair cards (over cards) on the final card (6 outs): 6.7/1 (13%)
- A second pair with your kicker on the final card, when you hold the same pair as your opponent but are 'out kicked' (3 outs): 14/1 (7%)

BEFORE THE FLOP MATCH-UPS (EXPECTED VALUE)

This section shows you the expected value against your opponent of non-suited hands pre-flop. Remember, value and odds are just that, even if the percentages are massively in your favour you are not guaranteed a win on that particular hand, but value over all over a period of play which will show you a healthy profit eventually.

Pair versus pair
A♦A♥ vs K♣K♠: 81.3%–18.7%
A♦A♥ vs 6♣6♠: 79.8%–20.2%

Pocket Bullets versus Big Slick
A♦A♥ vs A♣K♠: 92.6%–7.4%
A♦A♥ vs A♣K♣: 87.9%–12.1%

Pocket Bullets versus connectors
A♦A♥ vs J♣T♠: 82.0%–18.0%
A♦A♥ vs J♣T♣: 78.3%–21.7%
A♦A♥ vs 6♣5♠: 80.6%–19.4%
A♦A♥ vs 6♣5♣: 76.9%–23.1%

Pair versus two overcards

T T♥ vs A♣K♠: 57.3%–42.7%

T T♥ vs A♣K♣: 53.9%–46.1%

6 6♥ vs A♣K♠: 55.4%–44.6%

6 6♥ vs A♣K♣: 52.1%–47.9%

J T♦ vs 2♣2♠: 54.0%–46.0%

J T♥ vs 2♣2♠: 51.2%–48.8%

Pair versus one overcard (dominated hand)

K K♥ vs A♣K♠: 70.0%–30.0%

K K♥ vs A♣K♣: 65.9%–34.1%

6 6♥ vs 7♣6♠: 64.2%–35.8%

6 6♥ vs 7♣6♣: 60.5%–39.5%

Pair versus one overcard

K K♥ vs A♣Q♠: 71.6%–28.4%

K K♥ vs A♣Q♣: 67.9%–32.1%

T T♥ vs A♣2♠: 71.1%–28.9%

T T♥ vs A♣2♣: 67.4%–32.6%

6 6♥ vs A♣2♠: 69.9%–30.1%

6 6♥ vs A♣2♣: 66.2%–33.8%

Dominated hands

A K♥ vs A♣Q♠: 74.0%–26.0%

A♦K♥ vs A♣Q♣: 69.7%–30.3%

A♦K♥ vs A♣6♠ 73.5%–26.5%

A♦K♥ vs A♣6♣: 69.2%–30.8%

A♦K♥ vs K♣Q♠: 74.2%–25.8%

A♦K♥ vs K♣Q♣: 69.9%–30.1%

A♦K♥ vs K♣7♠: 75.0%–25.0%

A♦K♥ vs K♣7♣: 70.7%–29.3%

Two overcards versus non-pair

A♦K♥ vs 7♣6♠: 61.5%–38.5%

A♦K♥ vs 7♣6♣: 57.7%–42.3%

One overcard versus non-pair

A♦2♥ vs 7♣6♠: 53.9%–46.1%

A♦2♥ vs 7♣6♣: 50.4%–49.6%

CONCLUSION – POKER ODDS

Knowing how to calculate your odds in Texas Hold'em is fundamental to becoming a solid poker player. If you've found these pages difficult to understand, don't worry. Keep playing, bookmark this chapter, and come back to it when you need a reminder on how properly to gauge and apply the odds. Like everything else, learning to do this takes time.

5 ♠

CHAPTER 5

POKER TELLS

5 ♠

POKER TELLS

TOP TEN TELLS IN LIVE POKER

What is a poker tell? A tell is any habit, behaviour or physical reaction that gives other players information about your hand. The following are tips supplied to PokerTop10 by the pros, and can apply to both novice and advanced players. Remember though that in poker there are many contradictions and exceptions to the rule, and that experienced pros will often give out false tells to fool novice players.

1. Watch the eyes. This is why many pros wear sunglasses or visors/caps when playing; they know that the eyes rarely lie. Many players, for example, can't help but stare at big hole cards, giving the game away through that little bit of extra time they spend peeking at them. A player looking to steal the pot may look to his left to see if the remaining players, who haven't yet acted, appear likely to fold. Or again, a player may question you about your hand, knowing how hard it is to 'look someone straight in the eyes' while being dishonest.

2. **Facial expression**. Many pros try to hide their entire face by wearing a cap and looking downwards. This is to avoid the classic stare-down that poker pros are famous for. Some may try to study *your* face for nervousness (indicating a weak hand), or even look for repetitive characteristics like a body 'tic'. You may show obvious unhappiness if your hand is weak, or, conversely, exude confidence if your hand is strong.

3. **Weak is strong, strong is weak**. In its most simplistic form, this usually applies to novice players but frequently applies to pros as well. Basically, players like to be actors, and when they have a monster hand they tend to look disinterested. For example: 'Oh, is it my turn to act?' or 'Oh I guess I will play such and such.' Alternatively, a player speaking louder while raising the pot, or trying to look intimidating, may be running a bluff.

4. Anxiety. People typically feel anxious when they're confronted by something unpleasant or threatening, or anticipating such confrontation. Psychologists call this the 'fight or flight' response, and it links back to the days when we were cavemen/women. Physical changes take place, including flexing of muscles, eye-pupil dilation, palpitating heart rate and a dry throat. In poker, when someone has a big hand they are typically ready for confrontation and can exhibit some of these characteristics. You may see the chest expanding abnormally, or notice the player's voice become slightly higher as he makes a comment. Some of the top players in the game stare at the vein on the top-side of an opponent's face, watching for signs of a change in blood pressure. During a bluff, a player may demonstrate anxiety, but, if he knows he will fold the hand if re-raised (i.e. opts for a nonconfrontational end), he may look quite comfortable.

5. **Trembling hands**. These are another by-product of anxiety. Beware of a player whose hands are shaking; it normally means he or she is holding a monster hand.

6. **Glance at chips**. It is common for players to snatch a glance at their chips if they connect with the board after a flop. This may be a subconscious reaction, but it shows that the player is already planning an attack.

7. **Second look on the flop**. Some players will take another look at their hole cards when, for example, the board is showing a potential three-card flush draw. Able to remember only that the two cards are of different suits, they are looking to see if one of them is connecting.

8. **Repetitive betting patterns**. Usually the most revealing tells are based on the way a player habitually bets during particular situations. Some, for example, may always 'check' when they have made the nuts; others may regularly fold after being re-raised.

9. **Body posture**. Some players show obvious

changes in their posture based on their attitude/hand strength. For instance, shoulders tend to drop/slump when a player is not feeling confident (indicative of a weak hand). Conversely, a player sitting very attentively and in an erect position may be suggestive of strength. A player who bluffs a lot sometimes leans forward in a confrontational manner ... and so I could continue. Remember, strong is weak and weak is strong!

10. **Chip stacking**. When you first sit down at a table, study the way players stack their chips. Although it is a generalisation, loose aggressive players typically maintain disorganised/sloppy stacks, while tight conservative players keep theirs well organised and neat.

ONLINE POKER TELLS

We've probably all seen poker professionals staring each other down, looking for subtle tells in high-stakes poker. This sort of player-to-player interaction has made live poker what it is today: an extremely popular spectator sport. As we've seen, the best players in the world believe they can get hints concerning their opponents' hands simply by watching the pulse in their neck, the way their face reacts to certain circumstances or even the way they put their chips into the pot.

When playing online poker, there's obviously no such face-to-face interaction. Some poker professionals claim this takes some of the skill out of the game, making it more a question of mathematics than of people. To some extent, this might be true; it's certainly the case that poker professionals who rely heavily on tells from their opponents seldom do well at online poker. However, I believe that online poker tells are still there; you just need to know where to look. In fact, if you look closely enough a whole new set of tells emerges. Watch out for the following three.

TIME BETWEEN ACTIONS

As with live 'bricks-and-mortar' poker, the time it takes your opponents to act may reveal something about the strength of their hand. For example, a long pause and a bet is usually a sign of strength, whereas a long pause followed by a check tends to be a sign of weakness.

Online poker brings an added feature that bricks-and-mortar poker rooms don't have: before it's your time to act you can click on buttons that will then automatically indicate your decision at the appropriate moment. For example, you can click on check/fold or bet/raise, and when your turn comes round the software will do just that. You will often see five people fold in less than a second because they've all clicked on the check/fold button.

You can deduce a considerable amount of information concerning the strength of your opponents' hands by observing whether they've clicked in advance on the check/fold or bet/raise buttons. For example, if you've just checked after the flop and someone behind you instantly does the same, you can bet they have a poor hand and have pre-clicked on the appropriate button. A bet in a future round is sure to get them to fold more often than not. Similarly, if you bet against someone and before you can blink they've raised you, it's highly likely that they've clicked in advance and have a solid hand. In this case, you'll obviously need a strong hand to keep going. These two tells are unique to online poker and both, I believe, are strong ones.

You can usually assume that players who *always* take a reasonable time to act are doing other things while playing – surfing the net, for example, or playing more than one game. Either way, they're not giving their full attention to each game, so you can often raise these players out of pots, particularly if they're tight.

THE CHAT-BOX

Online poker allows you to talk to other players in the chat-box. Here is the rule: generally, the more a person chats, the worse they are at poker. This is something I've observed to be true through hours of playing. Also, players that abuse other players in the chat-box tend to be very poor players. After all, why would a good player abuse a fish? The only thing this will achieve is getting the fish to leave the table. Sometimes these players are so poor they'll actually tell you in the chat-box what cards they have. It can be as obvious as 'I have trips and I don't want to be outdrawn by a flush again' or 'Come on diamonds'!

POSTING OUT OF POSITION

Another tell is players posting out of position. You get this in live games as well, but because there's so much more movement between tables in online poker it happens there more often. A player who posts out of position is nearly always a poor player. Similarly, those who delay posting until it's their big blind, or until they have the button, are usually good patient players. This is a particularly useful tell since it can give you a read on players before they even play a hand.

CONCLUSION

Before I close this chapter, I must offer a word of caution. Although I've generally found the above rules to hold, better opponents may vary their strategy in order to keep you guessing. Make sure, then, that you watch each opponent carefully to get an accurate read on them.

CHAPTER 6

POKER TRAPS

POKER TRAPS

POKER traps are rarely addressed in articles and publications as much as they should be. Every professional poker player is able to set, spot and avoid a range of traps, but most amateur players haven't the faintest idea they're about to get pounced on until it's too late. Ask any skilled player on an Internet site what they think of the other players they typically come across, and they'll all respond with the same answer: 'Terrible!' Of course, many online players are relatively new to the game, so they inevitably have much to learn, but what makes beginners so much worse than 'good' players if poker really is just a mental game, as so many claim? In short, the answer is *starting hand selection*.

Much of the appeal of poker lies in it being a game anyone can win, but this is only the case because anyone can be dealt a winning hand. Let's face it, it takes no skill to win when you're sitting with the right cards; even the village idiot could do that. But what happens when the cards aren't coming? The ability to play (or better, *not* to play) bad cards is what separates the men from the boys in poker. Anyone can act grand during the good times, a player's true character is only revealed when the going gets tough.

In the rest of this chapter, then, I set out some of the traps you need to be on the lookout for.

AVOID PLAYING BIG CARDS WITH SMALL KICKERS (AA5, KK9, QQ8, ETC.)

'Texas Hold'em is a game of top pair, top kicker.' So, at least, claims TJ Cloutier, one of the best and most successful poker players of all time. In other words, what Texas Hold'em comes down to is holding a big pair and being able to stand up against the other kickers on the table. If you want to take the pot in at showdown, make sure that your kicker is up to the job, or you'll find yourself straggling in pots you have no business being in.

IN THE BIG BLIND AND SMALL BLIND, LEARN TO FOLD AFTER THE FLOP

If you look at the poker hands page, with the stats of each hand, you'll notice that players in the big and small blind position don't fare very well, tending, as above, to be dragged into a pot that they have no business being in. If you hold A5, for example, and hit top pair on the flop with four more players to act, then if the person after you bets it's practically a no-brainer to fold this hand. Most tight players play AT or better, so, if any tight player is in the game with an Ace showing on the board and there are no straight or flush possibilities out, you should automatically know you are beaten.

PREMIUM HANDS – ONE OF THE HARDEST POKER TRAPS TO AVOID

Another skill of the best poker players is their ability to lay down a strong hand when faced with a decision. Most poor players, and plenty of average ones, will refuse to lay down a strong hand, even when all the alarm bells are sounding. If you're playing a no-limit game, in particular, and someone comes with an enormous raise when you've made top pair with top kicker, it's often worth dropping. Don't let a good hand blind you to the possibilities of two pairs or a set. Whenever there's a possibility of a flush or straight on the table, never completely discount someone holding just that.

KJ, KT, QT, JT – GETTING OUT OF HARM'S WAY IN EARLY POSITION (EP)

This is probably the trap that players who don't understand the importance of position in Texas Hold'em most commonly fall into. Most players assume that any two facecards are well worth playing, which is generally true. However, as games become higher limit or as you play against more skilled opponents, things will tighten up considerably, players typically then only play premium hands.

ACE–QUEEN: A QUICK WAY OUT THE DOOR

Dropping a hand like AJ is easy enough, but dropping AQ will break many a heart. Having the courage to do so, however, can save your bankroll in many a situation. This advice is geared more towards higher limits or rational games, where raises from players are usually a good indicator of strength.

Many tight players will only raise with three hands: AA and KK (to increase pot value) and AK (to narrow the field). These are first-tier pre-flop raising hands. Second-tier pre-flop raising hands would, in my judgement, be either QQ, JJ or TT with AQ. The majority of uncreative tight players lie in the first-tier. Tight players who are more experienced will often raise tier-two hands as well. Many top players will raise with all sorts of hands, but usually as a ruse to be tricky or due to the high-limit nature of the games they play.

Given these first- and second-group hands, let's stack up how well AQ matches up against them:

Group-one hands
AA vs AQ: 92% to 8%
KK vs AQ: 72% to 29%
AK vs AQ: 72% to 24%

Group-two hands
QQ vs AQ: 70% to 30%
JJ vs AQ: 58% to 43%
TT vs AQ: 58% to 43%
AQ vs AQ 57% to 43%

I don't have enough bad things to say about people who play pocket pairs as if they are guaranteed winners. While pocket Jacks and Tens are both decent hands as far as pocket pairs go, they are still only a pair of Jacks or Tens, whichever way you look at it. Middle and low pocket pairs only work well when they are heads-up or if the flop comes up with nothing. When you are heads-up, you can play the game knowing you've already paired up, even if overcards fall on the table. With some trickery, you can even occasionally get a player who has a high pair to fold. In a full game, though, never ever count on this.

My personal preference is almost never to raise JJ or TT unless there are few limpers and I'm in a late or early position where I can focus on keeping people out. If you end up with four callers in a pot with you, JJ and TT quickly become worthless if an overcard falls. If action continues in such situations, you should routinely fold these pockets. Some tricky players will check-raise you if you show aggression from pre-flop to the flop, but, if you're up against unsophisticated players, you're surely beaten.

THE BOARD BOTH GIVETH AND TAKETH

These traps will be easily recognised by any seasoned player, but it will probably take you longer to learn them. Believe me, though: once you've been seriously burned by them, you'll soon commit them to memory.

WHEN THE BOARD PAIRS, A FULL HOUSE (OR QUADS) IS THE BEST HAND, NOT ACE FLUSH

A classic beginner's mistake is having an Ace-high flush and going toe to toe with some 'fool' who, surely, can only be betting on a King-high flush on a paired board. Of course, when that 'fool' flips over a full house, our beginner is absolutely devastated. While this doesn't mean you need to slam on the brakes every time the board pairs and you have an Ace-high flush, you do need to realise, should the going get heated, that your opponent holding a full house is a real possibility.

DRAWING HANDS – SOMETIMES A TRAP IS WAITING TO HAPPEN

Many new players attempting to study the game have a general understanding of pot odds and what type of hands to draw on, but they'll often think they've correctly understood the pot odds when, in fact, they haven't. As a result, they indulge in horrendous draws that are bound to lose in the long run. So pay attention here.

FLUSH/STRAIGHT DRAWS – DRAWING ON THE FLOP VERSUS THE TURN

In a *no-limit* or *pot-limit* game, you can make a serious mistake by drawing to a flush or open-ended straight (from now on, for the sake of brevity, whenever I refer to a flush draw, I'm referring to an open-ended straight as well). If the pot stands at $200 and the big blind swings in with a pot-sized bet of $200, then at that moment you are getting 2:1 pot odds should you call the pot. Many players will assume they're on a 2:1 draw here to hit their flush by the river, so they'll call, but *this is, in fact, an incorrect assumption to make*. In reality, though, you are on a 2:1 draw to make it by the river; if you don't hit your flush on the turn then you are actually a 4:1 underdog to hit your flush on the river. Thus, if the pot has risen to $600 on the turn, and the big blind comes in with another pot-sized $600 bet, you're still getting 2:1 pot odds, but your drawing odds are 4:1. This means you should definitely fold here and *should have folded on the flop as well*! If you're going to make a pot-sized bet on the turn, there's no way you want to be calling with 2:1 pot odds on a 4:1 drawing hand.

In summary, only go on flush draws in no-limit or pot-limit if you know that your opponents won't be making substantial bets on the turn that make your pot odds incorrect to draw on. You've been warned.

DRAWING TWO OVERCARDS WITH AN ACE

Another trap waiting to happen is drawing two overcards with an Ace. A two overcard draw is when you hold two cards greater than the board and are looking to pair either one, but otherwise have no other outs. This gives you six total outs, for a 3.2:1 draw. Probably the most common two overcard you'll see is when players call AK to the river after the flop has completely missed. They stick in for this overcard draw because they hate to see their AK go to waste. Personally, I've never been a big fan of drawing solely to hit overcards.

GETTING IN OVER YOUR HEAD

We've all been in the situation of making a large bet into the pot when holding a mediocre or strong hand (but not a monster), only for an opponent to come raising back. This is the sort of moment that makes your stomach churn and head begin to hurt. Learning whether or not to drop those cards is one of the most difficult things in the game, but also one of the most beneficial. Fooling yourself into the notion of being 'pot-committed' is, in my opinion, one of the biggest poker mind traps you can fall into.

THERE'S NO SUCH THING AS POT-COMMITTED IF YOU KNOW YOU'RE GOING TO LOSE

I find the idea of calling down a pot when you know you're beaten truly amazing. If you're in danger of getting knocked out of a tournament but are still in a good enough position not to get blinded out in the next few hands, you need to fold hands rather than get beaten, regardless of how many chips you've already put into the pot. If you have genuine doubts about a situation and are getting true pot odds then it's reasonable to call, but don't ever be the sort of player who says 'I was committed' when, in reality, you weren't. So often, it's just an excuse for making bad calls.

OVERBETTING YOUR HANDS

One way to keep out of those pot-committed situations is to not pot-commit yourself in the first place. Of course, sometimes you just can't avoid situations, but at other times you'll probably be given some warning signs that should prevent you from stepping into a trap.

OVERAGGRESSIVE PRE-FLOP BETTING IN A NO-LIMIT OR POT-LIMIT GAME

The standard self-trap is overbetting in a no-limit or pot-limit game. The blinds are 15/30 and you've gone gung-ho with those notoriously difficult pocket Jacks and bet 400 into the pot when there were only 50 there to start with. A tight player has moved all-in and you've got 300 more chips to call. If you do so, you're almost certainly dead, but, if you fold, your stack will be severely cut. It's much wiser to bet the current pot amount or, if there are only few players, three times the big blind amount. Thus, if you're under the gun (i.e. the first player to act in a round) and the blinds are 15/30, bet 90 up front. If you're late in the game and the blinds are very big, you can even bet two to two-and-a-half times the blind and have the same effect.

BETTING ON THE RIVER

Bets on the river are unique in that they're generally value bets (also known as 'bluffing' by the time you're on the river) instead of field-narrowing bets. What this means, then, is that you should only bet the river when you're confident you've the best hand in the game. How do you know you've got the best hand? That's a good question, and the answer, of course, is that you don't, but most of the time, based on the type of player calling you down, you should have a general idea of what you're up against. A tight player calling you down is a cause for concern if there are no apparent draws on the table, because it means he probably holds top pair. When a loose player calls you down, the chances are that he has a weak hand, *but never simply assume that's the case.*

When in doubt, a check on the river is always a safe play if you are last to act. Many times, your opponents will be holding busted draws on the river, and you can't extract value from those who were going to fold. I should add, though, that, against tricky opponents, a check can sometimes actually backfire against you, inducing another player to attempt a bluff. Against some opponents, at least, if you're willing to call their bet on the river, you may as well go ahead, betting the maximum amount you feel comfortable with and putting the decision back on their shoulders.

BLUFFING THE PERPETUAL CALLER

'How the hell did he steal that with 7-2 off-suit!?' When you come up against an inveterate caller (known in the game as a 'calling station', you're almost inevitably going to end up asking a question like that at some stage. I've done so numerous times myself, unfortunately. Knowing when to bluff is a direct off-shoot of identifying your opponents, and too often I've seen an otherwise good player try to make an all-in move against a calling station, only to see the latter stay in with the lowest pair on the board and end up winning. Your average player, who thinks he knows a lot about poker, will react with disgust and wonder how the hell an opponent could even consider calling them on a raise like this. What they don't realise is that they were the ones making the mistake by trying to bluff someone who they knew was a habitual caller. Some people just don't fold even when the train is coming, so against such people make sure you really do have a train, OK?

MENTAL POKER TRAPS

In reality, poker is a mental game, so it pays you to watch your own mindset if you are to avoid potentially expensive blunders.

NOT RESPECTING YOUR OPPONENT – A BAD MISTAKE TO MAKE

First, let me get things clear: it's one thing to consider someone a weak or bad player, but quite another not to respect their play. If you bet on a top pair and a weak player calls you with two spades on the table, you'll react differently depending on your mindset. If you respect your opponent, your reaction may be something like: 'I know he's weak, so he could have any pair, any kicker, with a good chance of a flush.' Your reaction if you don't respect him, though, could be: 'This guy is a total fish. I've bet big with top pair, so why doesn't he just fold now?' The key difference between these two mentalities is that, in the first one, you're thinking logically about what kind of hand your weak opponent may be holding and why he's calling. In the second, you're just thoroughly fed up that he's pursuing yet another hopeless draw, and you're itching to bet him out of the pot. You're thinking with your ego instead of your brain and it'll cost you dear when you fail to pick up on that completed backdoor straight or other dubious draws.

TRYING TO SAVE A POT WITH OVERAGGRESSION

There are some situations when, to borrow the well-used words of Mike Sexton, from the World Poker Tour, 'the only way to win this pot now is to bluff at it!' You know what I'm talking about … You have AK and have raised the pot $500 pre-flop. You've got two callers and you're under the gun. The flop misses you completely but, knowing you carry a tight table image with you, you want to scare off your opponents by seeming to have AA, so you bet a hefty $1,000 more into the pot. The first player drops immediately but the second person calls. 'Oh blast,' you scream mentally, wondering what kind of hand this 'fool' can be holding. The turn yields nothing and you've already got $1,500 or half your stack in the pot. Thinking frantically, you realise you've invested too much money to let this pot go down. You must outplay your opponent, and the only way to do so is with a huge $2,000 bluff. You move all your chips in with your unpaired AK and hold your breath. After a tense second, you groan as your opponent flips over QQ and knocks you out.

That was an example of overaggression. Sometimes you need to know when you're beaten – not at showdown, but on the turn or river. It hurts but, when you know you can no longer salvage the pot, you might as well check and fold it down. Yes, it's a huge blow to the ego when you've dumped a ton of money into the pot, led the way pre-flop and then in flop itself, only meekly to fold when your opponent gleefully comes at you, but at least then any money you save can go towards your continuation in the tournament or into your bankroll.

I'm not saying never bluff an opponent. Bluffing is a good and required part of the game, but trying to take down a pot by force when your opponent holds a decent hand is suicide.

CHAPTER 7

FREE MONEY!

FREE MONEY!

HOW TO MAKE MONEY FROM DEPOSIT BONUSES

Poker sites regularly offer deposit bonuses of 20 to 25 per cent to entice new players on to their sites. If you deposit $100, you get credited an extra $20–25 as a bonus, subject to you playing the requisite number of hands. By following the strategy laid out previously you should win handsomely, so it is obviously of great benefit to take maximum advantage of these deposit bonuses when they are offered. The number of requisite hands is usually seven times the deposit bonus amount. For example, to earn the bonus of $20, you must see around 140 hands. Always maximise on the highest level of deposit bonus offered. For example, if the maximum deposit bonus of 20 per cent is $100, then you should deposit $500. You will then have to see 700 hands in order to earn the $100 bonus. Many different poker sites offer monthly deposit bonuses, which means you can play them in turn and make more than $500 per month. Take full advantage of this free money!

HOW TO MAKE MONEY FROM POKER SITES WITHOUT EVEN PLAYING A HAND!

In poker jargon, it's called getting 'rake back'. In every hand you play, the house takes about 10 per cent of each pot. This is called 'the rake'. However, if you sign up for a 'rake back' programme, then you get part of the rake the house takes for every single hand you see. Think of it like a credit card with cash–back or a comp from the casino. Most 'rake back' programmes give you back 20–25 per cent. For example, if you play 5/10 Limit Hold'em, you would get about $.05 for every hand that you see (not play). So, if you see 1,000 hands in a week, you would get $50 back!

PokerLetter.org offer rake back of 25 per cent, but, in order to qualify, you need to open a special rake back account at Empire Poker and see at least 1,000 hands. (PartyPoker does not allow rake back.) PokerLetter.org manages hundreds of rake back accounts and their highest rake back player earns over $5,000 per month just from rake. How? He sees 40,000 hands of $15/$30 per month playing full-time at four tables. If you play regularly, why leave money on the table? I would urge all serious players to sign up for a 'rake back' programme.

The key to maximising profits from a rake back account is to play super tight, seeing around 18 per cent of flops. Why? You get paid to see a hand, not to play it. So you can wait patiently for premium hands and still make money while you wait.

CHAPTER 8

HOW TO SPOT CHEATS AND AUTOPLAYING ROBOTS ON THE INTERNET

HOW TO SPOT CHEATS
AND AUTOPLAYING ROBOTS
ON THE INTERNET

IF two people decide to play poker on the same Internet table, they can very easily share each other's cards by telephone, SMS or text. Knowing what each other holds gives cheats an immense advantage over the other players, and they will be able to collude in order to raise and re-raise other players out of pots, even though they may not necessarily hold good cards. One will also be in a position to raise, and then get the other friend to re-raise weak hands to steal the blinds from the other players. If one of them hits a good hand, the other can raise for them, in order to trap other players after they've called into committing more money. One can then call or re-raise to increase the pot further. However, this activity is strictly illegal and, if anyone gets caught, they will forfeit all the money in their poker account.

With tens of thousands of players on the tables of the larger poker sites on the Internet, there are always colluders, and this activity is very difficult for the poker sites to monitor. This is an area that needs addressing and policing, and is something every player on the Internet should be aware of. If you notice that two players are often playing hands together, make a note of their handles, and report the matter to the poker site as soon as possible. Be smart and on guard at all times, especially when playing on the higher-stakes tables, where cheats are most likely to be found playing. Fortunately, all cheats are out to make a quick buck, so it's not too difficult to spot them. Most are losers, desperately looking for some way to win (or lose less).

When, in the course of writing this book, I interviewed Mark Griffin, one of the high-profile Internet players featured earlier, I asked him how he could tell that the other players are real, and not computer-generated phantoms with the odds stacked in their favour. He was taken aback, and swiftly defended the bona fide credentials of the sites. 'These are real players, all right. A seasoned player would know if they weren't pretty quickly … If they are dummies,' he continued, 'they sure know how to chat!' This is an oblique reference to the chat-box facility that appears onscreen, via which players and observers pass remarks and comments to each other, not all of which are complimentary after a big hand has just been decided.

Recently, however, an avalanche of information has come to light, revealing that autoplaying robots do exist and have infiltrated some of the best-known online poker sites. Controlled, typically, by 'WinHoldEm', the first commercially available autoplaying software, it is possible now to buy a robot into a game, and he will play and run the numbers for you, knowing, statistically, when to play and when to fold. Set the robot on to autopilot, and it will win real money for you while you sleep. Flick on to Team

Mode and you can collude with other humans running WinHoldEm at the table. The invasion of the robot players is a concern. Of course, like any other player, they can lose if their hands are bad enough or their opponents sufficiently smart, so the poker sites loudly proclaim that automated play is no big deal. At the same time, however, they are fighting back by quietly scanning for and closing down suspicious accounts. PartyPoker, for example, claim they are ensuring no robots can infiltrate their site. The best way, however, to find out if the game you're playing in is clean is to start a chat session with all the players at the table. Better still, keep a note of the user handles of players you have already played against, and choose tables where you know the identity of your opponents.

And finally, just in case you haven't worked it out yet, the poker sites are on bet to nothing here. They make their money on what is called the rake, a small percentage taken out of every winner's pot. They have no risk, unlike a regular casino. They win on every hand that is played.

CHAPTER 9

LEGAL MATTERS

THE GAME OF POKER

PARTYGAMING – FLOATATION AND OPPOSITION

The Internet poker firm PartyGaming has floated on the London Stock Exchange, and as I write this it is valued as high as some of the biggest companies in Europe. But, despite being a listed company, PartyGaming will contribute a tiny 6 per cent rate of tax to the Treasury because it is registered in Gibraltar. It will also be exempt from new gambling laws intended to protect children and other vulnerable people becoming hooked on online gaming sites. The firm, which owns the world's biggest online poker website, PartyPoker.com, announced that it was expected to be valued at 5.5 billion pounds when it floated. That's right, 5.5 billion pounds! That's similar to Marks & Spencer, which was established in 1884, 113 years before PartyGaming.

The floatation of 23 per cent of its shares was expected to make its four founders multimillionaires. And the company's 1,100 staff, from Indian call-centre workers to head-office staff in Gibraltar, will be given 308 million pounds in shares, averaging £281,000 per employee. But the listing has brought criticism that gambling companies are able to invade Britain without being accountable to UK laws. The *Daily Mail* newspaper has led the way in campaigning for the new gambling laws to be tightened including helping reduce the number of Las Vegas-style mega-casinos in the UK from dozens to just one. And the US Justice Department has warned that online gambling can encourage fraud and money-laundering and would like to shut down some of the websites.

Jonathan Lomax of the Salvation Army has said,

'We are very concerned at the explosion of Internet gambling sites ... Gambling online has the potential to become very addictive and it is important that people understand this and that gambling sites ensure they adhere to the highest standards of social responsibility.' Then, in a reference to the passing of the Gambling Act, through which Internet gambling sites can register in the UK, he went on, 'They should commit to doing that, submit themselves to regulation and taxation, and prove that they care about some of the vulnerable people who end up addicted to gambling.'

Tory trade spokesman David Willetts has added, 'Britain should be a place that attracts companies from around the world to register here and pay their taxes here. It is important that gambling laws are properly regulated, and important that the British authorities are properly able to control and regulate gambling companies operating in the UK.'

PartyGaming was set up in 1997 by Indians Anurag Dikshit, 32, and Vikrant Bhargava, 33. One of its other owners, Ruth Parasol, made millions in the 1990s by setting up premium-rate adult phone chatlines and websites. She and her husband, Russ DeLeon, both Harvard law graduates, deal with the legal side of the company. Formerly known as iGlobalMedia, the company owns and runs the world's biggest online poker brand, PartyPoker, which has more than a million users with an average of 70,000 playing at any one time. It also owns other gambling sites such as StarLuck Casino and PartyBingo. The firm makes money by taking commission on the amount staked. Pre-tax profits in the year to 31 December 2004 were 204.6 million pounds, up from 49.1 million the previous year.

Chief executive Richard Segal, who led leisure group Rank's bid to operate the National Lottery a decade ago and later ran Odeon cinemas, said the results were 'further evidence of the growth in the online gaming market and specifically online poker'. He added, 'Our activities are not illegal. We take responsible gaming incredibly seriously. PartyGaming is a highly profitable and cash-generative business. Our focus will be to deliver attractive returns for our shareholders through a combination of the growth of the business and through the payment of dividends.'

Segal has been joined by Michael Jackson, chairman of accounting software firm Sage, who will fill the same job at PartyGaming – in so doing, he is holding the job at two FTSE 100 companies, which has raised questions as to whether this is in breach of corporate governance guidelines. It is reported that he has successfully negotiated a three year contract as Chairman. If this is true it would appear contrary to guidelines that state that a non-executive chairman of a FTSE 100 company must not have a contract that is longer than twelve months. Jackson will net three million pounds for three years in the job. Some shareholders at Sage expressed concern over his new role.

Meanwhile, it has just emerged that PartyGaming faces the threat of legal action under the Canadian Criminal Code. Canada is an important market for the group, but there are doubts there over whether the firm's gaming licence is legitimate. The group's prospectus reveals 'directors have been advised that the extent of the group's operations and presence in Canada may be sufficient for criminal or civil action to be taken'. The group's gaming licence was issued by the Kahnawake Gaming Commission in Canada. But the company has now conceded that there were serious doubts at a federal level as to whether this commission had the authority to issue such a licence. There are also no guarantees that a second licence will be issued. To reduce this risk, PartyGaming is moving its server centre to Gibraltar from Canada's Mohawk Territory. The casino and bingo server is being moved in August 2005 and the poker server by November. But it will retain a back-up operation in Canada. The firm has refused to disclose terms of directors' contracts and its level of insurance to cover litigation. Although the US Department of Justice considers online poker to be in violation of federal law, PartyGaming claims there is little risk of directors being arrested when they travel to America – a view not shared universally. PartyGaming maintains that executives regularly travel to the US. Other authorities take a more relaxed view. Although PartyGaming's prospectus warns that its Gibraltar gaming licence permits it to offer gambling services only in countries in which 'it is not illegal', the Gibraltar government, for the present at least, sees no reason to revoke the licence.

With 4.3 million people in Britain having gambled over the Internet, and with the online poker market expected to grow by 60 per cent this year, one would have thought PartyGaming would have ironed out these difficulties ahead of floatation.

IS ONLINE POKER LEGAL?

The direct answer to this question is: I don't know. I'm not a lawyer! Nothing in what follows should be seen as legal advice. It is simply a summary of the best information on this subject I've been able to find. Use it as you will.

Undoubtedly, increasing attention is being paid to the legal standing of online wagering in general. The first thing to understand, in relation to this, is that the skill game of poker is not the same as sports betting nor even 'random chance' casino games like craps and roulette. It may be treated the same eventually, but it may not. Legal precedent simply does not exist. At the time of writing, no person has been charged or brought to trial, let alone convicted and sentenced for playing online poker. But this does not guarantee one or more of these things will not happen in the future.

According to Professor I Nelson Rose, one of the world's leading authorities on gambling law: 'no United States federal statute or regulation explicitly prohibits Internet gambling, either domestically or abroad'. Still, the US government has taken the position that certain things are illegal and, more importantly, certain things are worthy of prosecution. The Wire Act is the statute most often cited as making online gambling a federal offence. The operative subsection reads:

Whoever being engaged in the business of betting or wagering knowingly uses a wire communication facility for the transmission in interstate or foreign commerce of bets or wagers or information assisting in the placing of bets or wagers on any sporting event or contest, or for the transmission of a wire communication which entitles the recipient to receive money or credit as a result of bets or wagers, or for information assisting in the placing of bets or wagers, shall be fined under this title or imprisoned not more than two years, or both.

Rose goes on: 'The first element of the Wire Act says that the statute applies only to an individual involved in the "business of betting or wagering" (not to a common player).'

The question of whether Internet sports betting is covered by the Wire Act seems to have been answered by the US Supreme Court's refusal to review the conviction of Jay Cohen. Whether online casinos and online poker cardrooms are covered under the Wire Act, which is specifically aimed at sports betting, is a different question. In February 2001, Judge

Stanwood Duval of the US District Court in New Orleans ruled that it did not: "'in plain language" [the Wire Act] does not prohibit Internet gambling "on a game of chance"' (text of Judge Duval's ruling). On 21 November 2002, the US Fifth Circuit Federal Appeals Court upheld Duval's ruling, stating:

> The district court concluded that the Wire Act concerns gambling on sporting events or contests ... We agree with the district court's statutory interpretation, its reading of the relevant case law, its summary of the relevant legislative history, and its conclusion.

The Appeals Court further states:

> Because we find neither the Wire Act nor the mail and wire fraud statutes may serve as predicates here, we need not consider the other federal statutes identified by the Plaintiffs ... As the district court correctly explained, these sections may not serve as predicates here because the Defendants did

not violate any applicable federal or state law.
The Appeals Court specifically cites Duval's
statement: ' plain reading of the statutory
language [of the Wire Act] clearly requires that
the object of the gambling be a sporting event or
contest.' This is very explicit language. You would
have to jump through a lot of mental hoops to
consider the playing of online poker to be 'a
sporting event'.

So, while the US Justice Department recently
stated that the Wire Act covers casino games in
addition to sports wagering, the Federal Appeals
Court has directly ruled that that interpretation
is not correct. This is not a small disagreement. It
is a direct contradiction that could well spur the
creation of new, 21st-century federal legislation
that actually deals with these issues.

One bill introduced by James Leach of Iowa
aims to inhibit the ability of citizens to gamble
online. It does nothing, however, to criminalise
actual gambling online. But other bills may be
introduced in the future with that goal.
Gambling regulation traditionally has been the
responsibility of individual states. For instance,

New York State Attorney General Eliot Spitzer reached a settlement with Citibank and PayPal regarding their involvement with online gaming. Some individual states have laws prohibiting any form of gambling online (or any gambling for that matter). That is a different issue from whether it is legal on a US federal level.

A key distinction exists on a federal level between bettors and those operators whose business it is to benefit from the actual making of wagers: 'engaged in the business of betting or wagering ... which entitles the recipient to receive money or credit as a result of bets or wagers, or for information assisting in the placing of bets or wagers ...' As long as players stay in the 'players' category and not in the in-the-business-of-wagering owners/bookies/ runners/agents categories, a significant difference in status exists. There are many ways to read the Wire Act, but only under the broadest interpretation could playing online poker be deemed illegal *in terms of the Wire Act*. In my opinion (which admittedly isn't worth all that much ... only the US

Supreme Court's view will matter unless new legislation is passed) playing online poker is not illegal for US citizens, in regards to federal law – unless it is a crime in an individual state, in which case the Federal Organized Crime Control Act of 1970 may apply. The Act makes it a federal crime for five or more persons to engage in a gambling business that is illegal under state law. Gambling online is definitely illegal in some states, but the Crime Control Act of 1970 does not apply to players. In addition, since the Crime Control Act does not refer to foreign commerce, it is hard to see how a case could be made that it applies to Internet gaming across multiple international borders.

Finally, in November 2004, the Caribbean island nation of Antigua and Barbuda won a World Trade Organisation ruling that United States legislation criminalising online betting violates global laws. In April 2005, the WTO Appellate Body affirmed the principal conclusions involved.

So, as long as online poker players do not participate in owning a share of the house rake;

as long as players only wager against each other; as long as players participate in the skill game of poker and do not bet on sports; as long as players obey state laws ... draw your own conclusions.

CHAPTER 10

THE NIGEL GOLDMAN TOP FIFTEEN ONLINE POKER TIPS

THE NIGEL GOLDMAN TOP FIFTEEN ONLINE POKER TIPS

1. Only risk 10 per cent of your bankroll in any one game.

2. Never play when drunk or tired – why do you think Vegas casinos serve out free drinks to their punters?

3. Ensure you are comfortable, and invest in a decent-sized monitor and wireless technology.

4. Consider a bogus identity – pretend you are a young girl player!

5. Create false alliances with other players.

6. Play two or more games at once: the bulk of your hands in any game will be poor, so this gives you more action and a better chance of hitting decent cards.

7. Watch out for instant action from other players – it probably indicates they're using pre-select buttons.

8. Most online players (especially in low-stakes games) are bad players, so there's no need to play too fancy.

9. Don't let other players bully you into playing or making decisions faster than you need to – ignore 'zzzzzzzzzz' comments in the chat-box if you're legitimately thinking through a hand.

10. Look out for value satellite competitions – many large prizes are won by online qualifiers.

11. Ensure that any credit card you have logged on with to play with is up to date.

12. Enrol with an online financial service agency such as Net Teller to help you process big wins.

13. Take a break, especially after a big win or heavy loss. Don't be shy about sitting out for a few minutes.

14. Remember, good players do most of their gambling on the flop.

15. Most of your profit will come from making the obvious correct moves.

11 ♣

11 ♣

CHAPTER 11

POKER
DICTIONARY

11 ♣

11 ♣

POKER DICTIONARY

ACTION: A fold, check, call, bet or raise. In certain situations, doing something formally connected with the game that conveys information about your hand may also be considered as having taken action. Examples would be showing your cards at the end of the hand, or indicating the number of cards you're taking at the draw.

ACTIVE PLAYER: A player still involved in the pot.

ADVERTISE: To bluff with the intention of being caught by the other players in order to entice them into calling a future bet that is *not* a bluff.

AGGRESSIVE ACTION: A wager that could enable a player to win a pot without a showdown; a bet or raise.

ALL-IN: When you've put all your playable money and chips into the pot during the course of a hand, you're said to be all-in.

ANTE: A prescribed amount posted before the start of a hand by all players.

BACKDOOR: When a player makes a hand he wasn't originally drawing at.

BAD BEAT: When a big hand is beaten by a long-shot draw.

BET: (1) The act of placing a wager into the pot on any betting round, or (2) the chips put in the pot.

BETTING THE POT: To bet the total amount of money currently in the pot.

BIG BLIND: The largest regular blind in a game.

BLIND: A required bet made before any cards are dealt.

BLIND GAME: A game which utilises a blind.

BOARD: (1) The board on which a waiting list is kept for players wanting seats in specific games. (2) Cards face-up on the table common to each of the hands.

BOARDCARD: A community card in the centre of the table, as in Hold'em or Omaha.

BOXED CARD: A card that appears face-up in the deck, where all other cards are face-down.

BRICKS-AND-MORTAR POKER: Poker played with real cards in a real casino, as opposed to virtual cards and a virtual casino online.

BROKEN GAME: A game no longer in action.

BURNCARD: After the initial round of cards is dealt, the first card off the deck in each round is placed under a chip in the pot, for security purposes. To do so is to burn the card; the card itself is called the burncard.

BUST OUT: Miss your hand completely, lose all your money.

BUTTON: A player who is in the designated dealer position. See DEALER BUTTON.

BUTTON GAMES: Games in which a dealer button is used.

BUY-IN: The minimum amount of money required to enter any game.

CALIFORNIA LOWBALL: Ace-to-five Lowball with a Joker.

CALL: To put money in the pot that's equal to the previous bet or raise.

CALLING STATION: A player who's next to impossible to bluff and who'll call almost any bet made.

CARDS SPEAK: The face value of a hand in a showdown is the true value of the hand, regardless of any verbal announcement.

CAPPED: The situation in limit poker in which the maximum number of raises on the betting round has been reached.

CASE CARD: The last card of a particular rank. For example, if you catch an Ace after the three other Aces are in the discards, then you have caught the case Ace.

CHANGE GEARS: Adjusting play from loose to tight, or vice versa.

CHECK: To waive the right to initiate the betting in a round, but to retain the right to act if another player initiates the betting.

CHECK-RAISE: To waive the right to bet until a bet has been made by an opponent, and then to increase the bet by at least an equal amount when it is your turn to act.

CHIP: A plastic token used in place of cash money.

COLLECTION: The fee charged in a game (taken either out of the pot or from each player).

COLLECTION DROP: A fee charged for each hand dealt.

COLOUR CHANGE: A request to change the chips from one denomination to another.

COMMON CARD: A card dealt face-up to be used by all players at the showdown in the games of stud poker whenever there are insufficient cards left in the deck to deal each player a card individually.

COMMUNITY CARDS: The cards dealt face-up in the centre of the table. These can be used by all players to form their best hand in the games of Hold'em and Omaha.

COMPLETE THE BET: To increase an all-in or forced bet to a full bet in limit poker.

CONNECTORS: Two cards or more of consecutive rank.

CUT: To divide the deck into two sections in such a manner as to change the order of the cards.

CUT-CARD: Another term for the bottom card.

DEAD CARD: A card that is not legally playable.

DEAD COLLECTION BLIND: A fee posted by the player having the dealer button, used in some games as an alternative method of seat rental.

DEAD HAND: A hand that is not legally playable.

DEAD MONEY: Chips that are taken into the centre of the pot because they are not considered part of a particular player's bet.

DEAL: To give cards to each player, or put cards on the board. Each deal refers to the entire process from the shuffling and dealing of cards until the pot is awarded to the winner.

DEALER BUTTON: A flat disc that indicates the player who would be in the dealing position for that hand (if there were not a house dealer). Normally just called 'the button'.

DEAL OFF: To take all the blinds and the button before changing seats or leaving the table. That is, to participate through all the blind positions and the dealer position.

DECK: A set of playing cards. In these games, the deck consists of either: (1) 52 cards in Seven-card Stud, Hold'em and Omaha; or (2) 53 cards (including the Joker), often used in Ace-to-five Lowball and Draw-high.

DISCARD(S): In a draw game, this either means to throw cards out of your hand to make room for replacements, or refers to the card(s) thrown away; the muck.

DOWNCARDS: Cards that are dealt face-down in a stud game.

DRAW: (1) The poker form where players are given the opportunity to replace cards in their hand. In some places, like California, the word 'draw' denotes the Draw-high version of the game, Draw-low being called 'Lowball'. (2) The act of replacing cards in the hand. (3) The point in the deal where cards are replaced is called 'the draw'.

EARLY POSITION (EP): Being one of those due to bet first in a multi-player game.

FACECARD: A King, Queen, or Jack.

FISH: Generally refers to a weak or careless player. Can also refer to a long-shot bet.

FIXED LIMIT: In limit poker, any betting structure in which the amount of the bet on each particular round is preset.

FLASHED CARD: A card that is partially exposed.

FLOORPERSON: A casino employee who seats players and makes decisions.

FLOP: In Hold'em or Omaha, the three community cards that are turned simultaneously after the first round of betting is complete.

FLUSH: A poker hand consisting of five cards of the same suit.

FOLD: To throw a hand away and relinquish all interest in a pot.

FOURTH STREET: The second upcard in Seven-card Stud or the first boardcard after the flop in Hold'em (also called the turncard).

FOULED HAND: A dead hand.

FORCED BET: A required wager to start the action on the first betting round (the normal way action begins in a stud game).

FREEROLL: A chance to win something at no risk or cost.

FREEZE OUT: A tournament that is played down to one winner and where no player can add more money to his original buy-in.

FULL BUY: A buy-in of at least the minimum requirement of chips needed for a particular game.

FULL HOUSE: A hand consisting of three of a kind and a pair.

HAND: (1) All a player's personal cards. (2) The five cards determining the poker ranking. (3) A single poker deal.

HEADS-UP PLAY: Only two players involved in play.

HOLE CARDS: The cards dealt face-down to a player.

INSIDE STRAIGHT: A straight with one of the inside cards missing; for example: T-J-K-A or 9-10-J-K (also known as a GUTSHOT STRAIGHT).

INSURANCE: A side agreement when someone is all-in for a player in a pot; to put up money that guarantees a payoff of a set amount in case the opponent wins the pot.

JOKER: The Joker is a 'partially wild card' in High-draw poker and Ace-to-five Lowball. In High, it is used for Aces, straights and flushes. In Lowball, the Joker is the lowest unmatched rank in a hand.

KANSAS CITY LOWBALL: A form of Low-draw poker also known as Deuce-to-Seven, in which the best hand is 7-5-4-3-2 and straights and flushes count against you.

KICKER: The highest unpaired card that helps determine the value of a five-card poker hand.

KILL (OR KILL BLIND): An oversize blind, usually twice the size of the big blind and doubling the limit. Sometimes a 'half-kill', increasing the blind and limits by 50 per cent, is used. A kill can be either voluntary or mandatory. A mandatory kill is typically enforced after a player wins two pots in a row at Lowball and other games, or scoops the pot in high–low split.

KILL BUTTON: A button used in a Lowball game to indicate a player who has won two pots in a row and is required to kill the pot.

KILL POT: A pot killed by the winner of the two previous pots, or the winner of an entire pot of sufficient size in a high–low split game. (Some pots can be voluntarily killed.)

LEG UP: Being in a situation equivalent to having won the previous pot, and thus liable to have to kill the following pot if you win the current pot.

LIVE BLIND: A blind bet giving a player the option of raising if no one else has raised.

LIST: The ordered roster of players waiting for a game.

LOCK-UP: A chip marker that holds a seat for a player.

LOWBALL: A draw game where the lowest hand wins.

LOWCARD: The lowest upcard required to bet at Seven-card Stud.

MISCALL: An incorrect verbal declaration of the ranking of a hand.

MISDEAL: A mistake on the dealing of a hand which causes the cards to be reshuffled and a new hand dealt.

MISSED BLIND: A required bet that is not posted when it is your turn to do so.

MUCK: (1) The pile of discards gathered face-down in the centre of the table by the dealer. (2) To discard a hand.

MUST-MOVE: In order to protect the main game, a situation where the players of a second game must move into the first game as openings occur.

NO-LIMIT: Betting structure where players are allowed to wager any or all of their chips in one bet.

NUTS: The best hand that can be made given the cards on the board.

OFF-SUIT: Two or more cards of different suits. Thus a Q♣ and J♠ would be termed QJ off-suit.

ON TILT: When a player plays poorly after losing one or more big pots.

OPENER: The player who made the first voluntary bet.

OPENER BUTTON: A button used to indicate who opened a particular pot in a draw game.

OPENERS: In Jacks-or-better Draw, the cards held by the player who opens the pot that show the hand qualifies to be opened. If, for example, you are first to bet and have a pair of Kings, the Kings are called your openers.

OPTION: The choice to raise a bet given to a player with a blind.

OUTS: The number of cards that will improve an inferior hand to a possible winner.

OVERBLIND: Also called oversize blind. A blind used in some pots that is bigger than the regular big blind, and usually increases the stakes proportionally.

OVERCARDS: Cards in the hand higher than any on the board.

OVERPAIR: A pair in the pocket in Hold'em that is higher than any card on the board.

PASS: (1) Decline to bet. In a pass-and-out game, this differs from a check, because a player who passes must fold. (2) Decline to call a wager, at which point you must discard your hand and have no further interest in the pot.

PAT: Not drawing any cards in a draw game.

PLAY BEHIND: Have chips in play that are not in front of you (allowed only when waiting for chips that are already purchased). This differs from table stakes.

PLAY THE BOARD: Using all five community cards for your hand in Hold'em.

PLAY OVER: To play in a seat when the occupant is absent.

PLAY OVER BOX: A clear plastic box used to cover and protect the chips of an absent player when someone plays over that seat.

POCKET PAIR: Two cards in a player's hand of the same rank; for example: Q-Q (Pocket Ladies) or K-K.

POSITION: (1) The relation of a player's seat to the blinds or the button. (2) The order of acting on a betting round or deal.

POT-LIMIT: Betting structure of a game in which you are allowed to bet up to the amount of the pot.

POTTING OUT: Agreeing with another player to take money out of a pot, often to buy food, cigarettes or drinks, or to make side bets.

PROPOSITION BETS: Side bets between players that are not related to the outcome of the hand.

PROTECTED HAND: A hand of cards that the player is physically holding, or that has been topped with a chip or some other object to prevent a fouled hand.

PUSH: When a new dealer replaces an existing dealer at a particular table.

PUSHING BETS: The situation in which two or more players make an agreement to return bets to each other when one of them wins a pot in which the other or others play. Also called saving bets.

RACK: (1) A container in which chips are stored while being transported. (2) A tray in front of the dealer, used to hold chips and cards.

RAINBOW: Three or four cards of different suits, particularly when they are dealt in the flop, are said to be rainbow.

RAISE: To increase the amount of a prior wager. This increase must meet certain specifications, depending on the game, to reopen the betting and count towards a limit on the number of raises allowed.

RAKE: A percentage fee charged by the house on every hand.

RAKE BACK: A percentage of the rake given back to players who have signed up for rake back.

RE-RAISE: To raise someone's raise.

ROCK: A player who plays only good hands and thus bets infrequently.

RUSH: A rapid succession of winning hands.

SANDBAG: Checking the probable best hand with the intention of raising.

SAVING BETS: Same as pushing bets.

SCOOP: To win both the high and the low portions of a pot in a split-pot game.

SCRAMBLE: A face-down mixing of the cards.

SETUP: Two suited decks, each with different-coloured backs, to replace current decks in a game.

SIDE POT: A separate pot formed when one or more players are all-in.

SHORT BUY: A buy-in that is less than the required minimum buy-in.

SHOWDOWN: The final act of determining the winner of the pot after all betting is completed.

SHUFFLE: The act of mixing the cards before a hand.

SHUT OUT: In a no-limit game, to force an opponent out with a bigger bet than he is willing to call.

SMALL BLIND: In a game with multiple blind bets, the smallest blind.

SNAPPED OFF: To get called when bluffing.

SPLIT POT: A pot that is divided among players, either because of a tie for the best hand or by agreement prior to the showdown.

SPLITTING BLINDS: When no one else has entered the pot, an agreement between the big blind and small blind to each take back their blind bets instead of playing the deal (chopping).

SPLITTING OPENERS: In High-draw Jacks-or-better poker, dividing openers in the hope of making a different type of hand. Imagine, for example, you open the pot with a pair of Aces, one of which is a spade, as also are the three other cards in your hand. If you throw away the non-spade Ace to go for a flush, you announce to the table, 'Splitting openers'.

STACK: Chips in front of a player.

STRADDLE: An additional blind bet placed after the forced blinds, usually double the big blind in size, or, in Lowball, a multiple blind game.

STRAIGHT: Five cards in consecutive rank.

STRAIGHT FLUSH: Five cards in consecutive rank of the same suit.

STREET: Cards dealt on a particular round in stud games. For instance, the fourth card in a player's hand is often known as Fourth Street, the sixth card as Sixth Street, and so on.

STRING RAISE: A bet made in more than one motion, without a declaration of a raise (not allowed).

STUB: The portion of the deck which has not been dealt.

STUD: Any form of poker with multiple betting rounds in which players are dealt a mixture of face-up and face-down cards.

STUCK: When a player is losing, he is said to be stuck.

SUCKER: A player who thinks he knows how to play, but has little chance of winning because of his ineptitude.

SUPERVISOR: A cardroom employee qualified to make rulings, such as a floorperson, shift supervisor or the cardroom manager.

TABLE STAKES: (1) The amount of money you have on the table. This is the maximum amount that you can lose or that anyone can win from you on any one hand. (2) The requirement that players can wager only the money in front of them at the start of a hand, and can only buy more chips between hands.

TELL: A mannerism of a player that gives opponents an indication of the strength of his hand or whether or not he is bluffing.

TIGHT PLAYER: A player who plays only strong hands.

TIME: An expression used to stop the action on a hand. Equivalent to 'Hold it!'

TIME COLLECTION: A fee for a seat rental, paid in advance.

TOKE: A gratuity. Commonly used in gambling as opposed to 'tip'.

TOURNAMENT: A poker competition, normally with an entry fee and prizes.

TRIPS: Three of a Kind.

TURNCARD: In Hold'em or Omaha, also called Fourth Street (i.e. the fourth card to be dealt).

UNDER THE GUN: The first player to act in a round.

UPCARDS: Cards that are dealt face-up for opponents to see in stud games.

WAGER: (1) To bet or raise. (2) The chips used for betting or raising.

WALK: Letting the blind win unchallenged.

WHIPSAW: The caller between two players who are both raising.